Exiting Your Business with Clarity

Aligning Your Business, Personal Finances, and Legacy for Success

Edward Barone

ISBN: 978-1-968247-03-4 (Digital)

ISBN: 978-1-968247-06-5 (Paperback)

Book Cover by 100Covers

Edited by Bailey Baack

1st Edition 2025

About the Author

Ed Barone joined the Evergreen Wealth Solutions team in 2018, bringing over two decades of experience in holistic wealth management. He currently leads the Evergreen Exits division. Ed is a Certified Business Exit Consult through the International Exit Planning Association and a Certified Mergers and Acquisitions Advisor through the Alliance of Mergers & Acquisition Advisors. Since 2000, Ed has served as a dedicated wealth manager, specializing in Business Exit Planning for privately held businesses and Institutional Asset Management since 2012. His commitment to excellence was recognized in 2023 when he received the "Excellence in Exit Planning Award" from the International Exit Planning Association, where he also serves as a valued member of their Leadership Council.

Acknowledgments

I sincerely thank the International Exit Planning Association and its Founder, John Leonetti, for their commitment to empowering business owners and Certified Business Exit Consultants. Their practical, experience-based education and comprehensive resources have been instrumental in equipping countless professionals with the tools needed to facilitate successful business transitions.

Contents

INTRODUCTION

The Impact of Exit Planning

Every business owner will one day leave their company. The only unknown is whether that exit will happen by design or by default. For many owners, their business is not just their greatest financial asset. It is also their identity, their legacy, and the center of their daily lives. Yet despite this reality, most business owners are unprepared for this inevitable transition.

Consider the statistics:

- **Emotional and Psychological Barriers:** The primary reason for the lack of planning is the emotional difficulty of confronting an exit. While 95% of owners acknowledge the importance of a transition, planning for it requires them to face the end of their professional identity, which is often tied to feelings of loss or an "association that something rewarding is coming to an end."

- **Procrastination and Lack of Urgency:** The statistic that 74% plan to transition in the next ten years suggests that the majority of owners view an exit as a future event, not an immediate priority. This mindset leads to procrastination, as they believe there is ample time to prepare—a belief that is often disrupted by unexpected events.

- **Unplanned Life Events:** The reality is that 50% of all transitions are not planned, but are instead forced by unforeseen circumstances like death, disability, or burnout. This highlights that many owners are forced into an exit on someone else's terms before they have had a chance to implement a plan.

- **Misconceptions and Focus:** The statistics also show that even after a sale, 70% of owners are dissatisfied. This dissatisfaction stems from a failure to prepare for life beyond the business or from exiting on unfavorable terms. This indicates that owners often prioritize the day-to-day operations and building the business rather than preparing for the personal and logistical complexities of their eventual departure.

In essence, the statistics reveal a common pattern: business owners recognize the importance of exit planning but are hindered by emotional reluctance and a tendency to prioritize immediate business demands over a distant future event. This leaves them vulnerable to unplanned exits and the regret that follows when a transition is not executed on their own terms.

Exit planning doesn't mean selling your company right away. It means being prepared so that whenever the transition comes, whether by choice or by circumstance, both you and your business are ready for the future.

A Case Study:
Why Preparation Matters

One business owner, Jon, came to his advisors with an offer in hand and was close to signing a letter of intent. On the surface, the deal looked attractive. After a thorough financial and estate review, the analysis showed the net proceeds would not support his family's goals or long-term plans. At age fifty, Jon had too much life ahead of him to accept a shortfall.

He walked away, regrouped, and invested the time to strengthen his company's value. Two years later, the same private equity firm came back to him with a stronger offer. This time, the deal closed quickly, on Jon's terms. He not only secured greater financial resources, but he also had the clarity to plan for life after the exit, and launched a new business that aligned with his long-term vision.

Jon's story underscores the essence of exit planning: Preparedness creates options. Without the planning process, he would have accepted an inadequate deal. With it, he achieved a better financial outcome, safeguarded his family, and charted a new legacy.

Whether you have an offer you're considering like Jon or you couldn't dream about walking away from your business, it's never too early to start thinking about exit planning. With thoughtful preparation, owners can maximize financial outcomes, safeguard employees, preserve legacies, and step confidently into the next chapter of their lives.

CHAPTER ONE

What Does Exit Planning Mean to You?

Exit Planning Is a Process, Not a Transaction

❧

Exit planning is often misunderstood. Many owners think it's only about selling a business or cashing out at the right time. In reality, it's about much more: clarifying what matters most, protecting the people who depend on you, and making sure your life's work carries forward with purpose.

The stories in this chapter show how unplanned events can force difficult decisions and how thoughtful preparation can turn those moments into opportunities. They remind us that a successful exit isn't just a transaction. It's a process that demands foresight, courage, and a clear vision of the future.

"Setting a goal is not the main thing. It is deciding how you will go about achieving it and staying with that plan." – Tom Landry

Bob's Story:
Learning to Delegate

Bob never thought he would need to plan his exit. For years, his identity was wrapped up in his business. He wore every hat— chief decision-maker, lead salesperson, operations manager—and the company depended on him for everything. Then his wife fell seriously ill and his world shifted overnight.

Suddenly, the numbers on a balance sheet didn't matter as much as the time he might not have with her. He decided it was time to sell and assumed he could manage the process himself. After all, he had built the company from scratch, so who could possibly understand it better than him?

Selling a business is not like selling a product or even a house. It requires a different set of legal, financial, and emotional skills that Bob didn't fully anticipate. Six months into trying to juggle running the company while negotiating the sale, his business began to suffer. Deals slipped. Operations lagged. The very thing he was trying to preserve was deteriorating.

Buyers, too, quickly noticed the risks. Without Bob, there was no company. Processes lived in his head. His leadership team wasn't truly empowered. Everything funneled back to him. For an outside buyer, that dependence was a red flag.

At last, Bob recognized that his way wasn't working. He engaged an investment banker and a team of advisors who helped him take a different approach. With guidance, he began to let go. He gave his Chief Financial Officer (CFO) real authority and encouraged his sales manager to lead. Slowly, his company began to look less like an extension of Bob and more like a business that could stand on its own.

When the deal finally closed, it was because the buyer saw strength beyond the owner. Bob walked away with not only financial security, but also with the peace of mind that his wife, his employees, and his company's future were secure.

Bob's journey shows why exit planning is more than a financial transaction. It is a process of creating transferability. Buyers do not want a business that collapses when the owner leaves. They want confidence in the systems, the people, and the culture that remain. For Bob, the act of delegating was about learning to release control so the company could move forward without him.

Joe's Story:
The Weight of Legacy

Joe's wake-up call came at a funeral. Standing at the graveside of his closest friend, he asked himself a sobering question: *"If I died tomorrow, what would happen to my wife and my employees?"*

For years, Joe assumed he would pass the business internally to his leadership team. They were loyal, hardworking, and had been by his side for decades. He saw them almost as family, and the thought of them carrying the company forward gave him comfort.

When he began planning in earnest, the cracks appeared. His team, while dedicated, didn't have the skillset required to step into ownership. Leadership and management are different from ownership, and the transition proved too great. Despite coaching and outside searches, Joe couldn't find a replacement who could fill his shoes.

This reality forced him to face a truth he had long resisted: An internal handoff wasn't possible. His dream of seeing "family" carry on the business had to give way to another path.

Eventually, Joe sold to one of his largest customers. It wasn't the scenario he had envisioned, but it aligned with what mattered most to him. The buyer committed to keeping operations in the same town, protecting jobs, and maintaining continuity for his employees. To seal the deal, Joe even offered favorable lease terms on his building, ensuring that the company—and the people he cared about—would remain rooted in the community.

Joe did not walk away with the highest possible price, he did walk away aligned with his values. For him, exit planning wasn't about squeezing every dollar from the sale. It was about knowing his true priorities and structuring the deal around them.

Joe's journey reveals another core truth about exit planning. It is as much about emotional readiness and legacy as it is about financial outcomes. Owners often start the process believing one path like family succession, employee buyout, or management transfer is the obvious choice. When tested against reality, those assumptions sometimes collapse. Exit planning helps you face those hard truths and choose a strategy that aligns with what matters most.

Chapter One in Practice

Bob's story was about learning to let go. Joe's was about redefining what mattered most. Both reveal the same reality: Exit planning is a process, not an event. It requires time, honesty, and a willingness to ask and answer difficult questions.

Reflection Questions

These questions don't have easy answers. Grappling with them before a crisis arises is what separates those who exit on their terms from those who are forced out by circumstance.

- What happens if I can't return to work tomorrow?

- Would my company survive without me?

- Do I value price above all else, or is my legacy more important?

- What will I do with my time once the business no longer depends on me?

Action Step

Take time to write down your top three priorities for your eventual exit. Don't worry about strategy yet. Focus on what matters most. Is it financial security? Protecting employees? Preserving legacy? Creating freedom for yourself? Once you have clarity on these priorities, the process of exit planning becomes less about fear of change and more about designing the future you want.

Sample priorities:

- I want to maintain my current lifestyle, buy a house in South Carolina, and leave $3 million to each child.

- The next owner must have a similar culture that values my employees.

_____

_____

CHAPTER TWO

Mental Readiness

"Why would I plan for change when I love what I am doing?"

❧

W hen you've poured decades of your life into building a company, it becomes more than work. It becomes part of who you are. Your business card is your identity. Your calendar is your structure. Your staff is your extended family. To imagine life without that rhythm feels foreign, even threatening. And yet, every owner eventually reaches a moment when they must ask: **Am I ready to step away? And what does that mean for me?**

Five Mental Hurdles of Exit Planning

#1. The Invisible Weight of Identity

Entrepreneurs often underestimate how much of their identity is tied to their business. They may say, *"I know who I am without this,"* but the truth often emerges after they step away. Suddenly, the phone doesn't ring. People stop asking for decisions. The respect and recognition once tied to ownership fades.

One owner, after selling, confided that he no longer knew how to introduce himself at social events. For years, he had been "the founder." Without that title, he felt stripped of significance. The money in his bank account didn't fill the void.

The hurdle: Separating who you are from what you own

The shift: Begin practicing detachment early. Introduce yourself in settings without mentioning your title. Pursue interests, hobbies, or community roles that give you identity outside of work. The earlier you create a life beyond your company, the smoother the transition will be.

#2. Fear of Mortality

Planning for an exit forces owners to confront the passage of time. For some, this feels uncomfortably close to admitting their own mortality. To write down a succession plan can feel like writing their own obituary.

One owner delayed exit planning for years, always answering, "in five more years." Deep down, he wasn't resisting the process. He was resisting the idea of aging, of change, of endings. When a health scare forced his hand, he realized too late that he had wasted the chance to prepare thoughtfully.

The hurdle: Equating exit planning with death or decline

The shift: Reframe the narrative. Exit planning is not about endings. It's about beginnings. It is about designing the next stage of life, one that can be rich with freedom, choice, and legacy. By shifting the focus from "what I'm leaving" to "what I'm creating," the fear of mortality loosens its grip.

#3. The Addiction to Control

For many founders, control is comfort. From day one, they've made every decision—hiring, strategy, finances, customer relationships. That instinct is part of what fueled their success. But when it comes time to exit, that same instinct becomes a liability.

Letting go feels like weakness. Delegating feels risky. Trusting others to carry the torch feels impossible. Yet without a team that can operate independently, the business loses value in the eyes of a buyer. The irony is painful. The very control that built the company is what reduces its worth when it's time to sell.

The hurdle: Fear that no one can run the business as well as you

The shift: Start small. Delegate a single major decision to a trusted manager and resist the urge to take it back. Document processes. Allow others to solve problems without your intervention. Over time, you will discover that the company not only survives, but often thrives when others are empowered.

#4. Family Expectations and Guilt

For many owners, the question of succession is tangled in family dynamics. Children may feel pressured to step into a role they never wanted. Spouses may fear the uncertainty of transition. Extended family may carry assumptions about inheritance, control, or legacy.

One owner, eager to keep his business "in the family," spent years grooming his daughter for leadership. Only after she finally confessed did he learn she had no passion for the work. She wanted her own career. The years of assumption strained their relationship and delayed a healthier plan.

The hurdle: Assuming family will—or should—take over

The shift: Have courageous conversations early. Ask family members directly about their interest and capacity. Be willing to hear "no." Protect relationships by separating business decisions from emotional expectations. A successful exit honors both family harmony and business continuity.

#5. The Illusion of Indispensability

Perhaps the most universal mental hurdle is this belief: "This business cannot survive without me." Owners convince themselves they are the glue holding everything together. While this belief can feel true, it often blinds them to the capability of their teams.

A client once said, "If I walked away for a month, the whole thing would collapse." At the urging of his advisors, he tested it. He left for two weeks, unplugged, and returned to find that not only had things not fallen apart, but his managers had solved issues with fresh ideas he never would have considered. That experience became the turning point that allowed him to finally imagine life beyond ownership.

The hurdle: Believing the business ends when you step away

The shift: Test your absence. Take extended vacations. Step back gradually and let your team lead. Watch the business operate without you. Each small experiment builds confidence that the company is, in fact, transferable.

Too often, owners avoid planning because they cannot imagine life after business. Without a vision of the next chapter, the void becomes paralyzing.

The solution is to dream again. Some find fulfillment in philanthropy. Others become mentors or advisors. Some explore long-neglected passions—travel, writing, teaching, art, or simply time with family. What matters is not the form, but the clarity.

Knowing what will fill your days brings comfort and purpose to the transition.

Chapter Two in Practice

Reflection Prompts

- In what ways is your identity currently tied to your role as owner?

- What fears arise when you imagine stepping away—loss of purpose, control, recognition, or something else?

- Which family assumptions about the business need to be clarified through honest conversations?

- What would excite you enough to get out of bed the day after your exit?

- How can you begin practicing detachment through delegation, outside pursuits, or intentional time away?

Action Step

Choose one mental hurdle you recognize in yourself and take a deliberate step to address it this month. That might mean delegating authority, having a family conversation, taking an extended break, or exploring a new pursuit outside of work. By negotiating these mental hurdles now, you prepare yourself not just to exit your business, but to enter the next stage of life with clarity, confidence and self fulfillment.

CHAPTER THREE

Financial Readiness

Getting Your Financial House in Order

❦

When it comes to exiting a business, most owners are confident they'll be ready when the time comes. They know what their company provides for income, they've worked with lenders and accountants, and they assume that when they're ready to sell, a buyer will pay a price that sets them up for the rest of their lives.

Reality often tells a different story. Financial readiness is about knowing with certainty what your business is worth, what you will actually net when the deal closes, and what you need for income for the rest of your life and for heirs. Without this clarity, even the most successful-looking sale can leave an owner vulnerable, anxious, or forced to reenter the workforce just to maintain their lifestyle.

The Value Gap in Real Life

Consider Michael, who owned a manufacturing business he'd built over thirty years. He believed the company was worth at least $10 million. In his mind, that figure would provide more than enough for retirement, travel, and leaving a legacy to his children.

When he finally engaged a valuation team, the results were sobering. His company was valued closer to $6.5 million. On top of that, once transaction costs, taxes, and debt obligations were factored in, his net proceeds would land under $4 million. That number wasn't enough to sustain his family's lifestyle or cover the estate plans he and his wife envisioned.

Michael had fallen into a common trap: mistaking his aspiration for reality. The gap between what he needed and what his business could deliver—his value gap—was nearly $3 million. Closing that gap meant recommitting to growth, delegating more to his management team, and investing in transferable systems that would drive up his eventual valuation.

The lesson here is that without knowing your true value and what you need, you can walk into a deal blind and walk out unprepared.

<h2 style="text-align:center">Gross vs. Net:</h2>
The Painful Surprise

Another owner, Linda, proudly accepted an $8 million offer for her technology services company. On paper, it looked like the windfall of a lifetime. Friends congratulated her on "cashing out." When the dust settled, the reality was harsher.

Her deal was structured with a significant earnout tied to performance benchmarks she no longer controlled. Taxes consumed more than she expected. Her accountant had warned her, but she hadn't fully grasped the impact of capital gains versus ordinary income tax. By the time legal fees and obligations were met, Linda walked away with just under $4.5 million in actual proceeds.

She admitted later: *"If I had understood the difference between gross and net, I would have approached the negotiation entirely differently.*" The big sale number may make headlines, but it's the net proceeds—the money you actually keep—that determine your financial future.

Estate and Legacy Planning:
Common Hurdles to Avoid

Financial readiness goes beyond what the owner needs personally. It extends into what happens after wealth changes hands. Owners often avoid estate planning because it forces them to confront uncomfortable questions: mortality, who inherits, how much, and under what terms? Families without a plan can be burdened by estate taxes, disputes, or poor financial stewardship.

One client, a widowed owner of a retail chain, realized late in her planning process that her children weren't equally capable of managing wealth. By setting up tailored trusts, she protected assets from creditors and provided structures that fit each child's circumstances. More importantly, she reduced potential conflict among heirs by making those decisions proactively rather than leaving them to chance.

The lesson here is that estate planning is essential for protecting relationships, ensuring continuity, and aligning wealth with values.

Owners who want to protect their future must confront several common hurdles directly:

- **Overestimating business value:** It's easy to assume your company will sell at the same earnings multiple as others in your industry. The reality is that every business carries unique risks that detract from value. Each balance sheet and profit-and-loss statement tells a different story.

Assuming your company is worth "what the neighbor's sold for" is a costly mistake.

- **Failing to diversify wealth before the sale:** For most owners, seventy to eighty percent of their net worth is tied up in the business. That level of concentration is risky. What happens if you die unexpectedly? Would the company hold its value without you, or would employees and loved ones bear the burden? By building wealth outside the business, you create income streams that not only protect your family but also allow for more flexible deal structures, such as buyouts over time, that can reduce overall tax exposure.

- **Lack of a succession strategy:** Few events devastate a company more than the sudden loss of an owner without a succession plan. I've seen both well-prepared and unprepared families navigate this situation, and the difference is stark. One widow I worked with, Joanne, lost her husband— a business owner—just a year before COVID struck. With no diversification of wealth and no succession plan, the business was forced to close. The business value collapsed by seventy percent, leaving Joanne, at age 65, still working. With foresight, that outcome could have been prevented.

- **Neglecting estate planning:** A thorough estate review before listing your business can yield enormous tax savings for your heirs. One client with a $50 million company reclassified shares and used the federal exemption strategically, reducing estate taxes by $12 million. Planning ahead protected not only the family's wealth but also the owner's legacy.

- **Overlooking charitable planning:** Philanthropy can be part of your exit plan, but it requires thought. Which assets will provide the greatest benefit for both your cause and your tax picture—business interests, real estate, retirement accounts, or stocks? Choosing the right asset can maximize impact and minimize tax.

Financial readiness requires understanding all aspects of your lifestyle, income sources, and goals for heirs and charities. Tools like the Business Exit Readiness Index (BERI) assessment provide clarity on where you stand, but it's the willingness to act—seeking professional advice, setting realistic targets, building wealth outside the business—that determines whether your exit secures your future or exposes you to regret.

The Business Exit Readiness Index

At Evergreen Exits, we have clients take the Business Exit Readiness Index survey early in our planning process because we want to understand where they fall mentally and financially. What type of business owner are you regarding financial readiness and mental readiness? Let's bring this all together to help you determine the appropriate exit strategy.

What comes out of the assessment is ranking a business owner in four quadrants:

- **Bottom left quadrant:** Low financial, low mental readiness
- **Top left quadrant:** High financial readiness, low mental readiness

- **Bottom right quadrant:** Low financial, high mental readiness

- **Top right quadrant:** High in both financial and mental readiness

BERI Quadrants

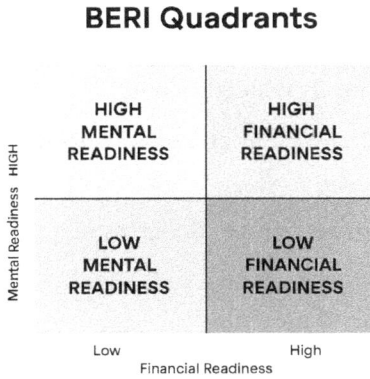

Our goal is to get you to the top right quadrant. When you reach the top right, high financial and mental readiness, you get to pick and choose your buyer and who you want to own your business. The bottom right quadrant represents someone who's just burnt out; financial readiness doesn't matter, mental readiness doesn't matter, but something has happened and you just need out.

Understanding where you are helps us walk you through the exit paths and options, determining which ones align with your goals. This framework guides us toward the five exit strategies and the pros and cons of each, helping you understand which cons you're willing to live with and which pros mean the most to you.

"Someone's sitting in the shade today because someone planted a tree a long time ago." – Warren Buffett

Chapter Three in Practice

Reflection Prompts

- What is the gap between what your business is worth today and what you truly need to net?

- How much of your wealth exists outside of your business?

- Have you modeled your net proceeds after taxes, fees, and deal structure—not just the gross sale price?

- Where would the BERI assessment place you right now financially and mentally?

- Have you created a plan to protect your heirs and reduce the tax burden on your estate?

Action Step

Scan this QR code to take the Business Exit Readiness Index:

CHAPTER FOUR

The Five Exit Paths

Understanding Your Options

❦

In order to gain clarity when working with business owners, we start by looking at the five exit strategies. Usually early on in the conversation, they've identified one that they'd like to pursue, but they really don't know if it's feasible until we have deeper conversations.

Keeping your business legacy going, taking care of your employees, and making sure the business is going to stay in the community are all emotional pieces of transitioning out of your business.Most business owners would like to see an internal transfer happen. The reality is that's not always feasible.

Think back to the earlier case study of Joe who really wanted to do an internal transfer but ultimately did an external transfer. Why was that? He didn't have family to take over. He did have four key leadership team members, but he ultimately identified that they didn't have the skill sets needed to be owners.

Internal Transfer:
The Deep Questions

You really have to dig down deep when you're looking at an internal transfer. Just because you have great managers doesn't mean they're great leaders. The skill set of an owner differs from the skill set of a manager. You must evaluate if a manager can be mentored to become an owner.

The next question is, can they be trained in those skill sets? Often, it is challenging. Sometimes internal transfers involve families, and that sparks even more questions:

- Do they really want it or do they feel obligated?
- Do they want it because you're going to transfer it to them free of cost?
- Can I lend to this business?
- Do I need to hold collateral for this business because it's higher risk? How much collateral?

I worked with one family where there were five people in the second generation, but two really didn't want to be in the business. We worked out a win-win deal structure which bought them out of the business at a discounted value, but tax-free. Then there was planning for the remaining three children.

A third-generation member of the family had been working in the business for years and wanted to take it on. I recommended that they should not just give it to the third generation, and that the potential successor should have to go to a bank and take out a loan for 10% or 20% of the value. Because that will let you know if they really want it. By not having to do that, you're robbing them of valuable education.

When they went back to their family member with those conditions, the third-generation member said they didn't want it. Three months later, she left the business and found a job. Now there are no hard feelings between one generation and the next. They were offered it, didn't want it, and decided to move on.

This chapter will go through the pros and cons of each strategy, and I think it's important for business owners to understand those strategies. Those pros and cons will vary based on the owner and based on the buyer. They're really not one-size-fits -all.

External Sale:
The Emotional Challenge

Some challenging emotions of an external sale include:

- Do they have the same employee culture?
- Are they going to take care of my employees?
- Are they going to keep the business here in the community long term?Or is this a short-term stint?

You also have to understand that some of those external sales come with different challenges. Are you going to be able to separate from the company immediately? What does that look like?

It's very rare that any business owner walks away with 100 percent of the sale at the closing. I've seen business owners have positive experiences with external sales and I've also seen some not-so-positive experiences. Understanding the buyer and what they expect from you upon your exit is really critical.

Typically, when you look at selling to a third party or a private equity firm, you can walk away with more money. The exit is probably going to be quicker than a family or management buyout exit as a strategy to leave the company. You will stay engaged at some level with each type of transaction. The question is the level of engagement and how long that engagement lasts.

The Five Exit Strategies Detailed

Internal Strategies
1. Family Transfer

A family transfer is one of the internal exit strategies where the ownership of a business is transitioned to children or other family members. Instead of selling to outside buyers, the goal is to keep the business within the family and preserve its legacy.

Key characteristics of a family transfer include:

- **Ownership Transition:** Shares or control are passed to family members, often children, either gradually or at once.

- **Financing:** It often involves seller financing (the exiting owner finances part of the purchase) or a gradual transition of ownership to make it affordable for the next generation.

- **Capability Assessment:** Success requires an honest evaluation of whether family members have (or can be trained in) the skills to manage, lead, and own the business.

- **Tax & Estate Planning:** These transfers may involve estate planning tools, such as trusts, to minimize taxes and protect family wealth across generations.

- **Risks & Considerations:** Challenges include family dynamics, unequal interest among siblings, and the possibility of lowering business value compared to an external sale.

In short, a family transfer prioritizes legacy and continuity over maximum sale price, often trading some financial upside for emotional and generational goals.

Pros	Cons
Preserves Legacy – Keeps the business within the family and honors the founder's vision and values.	**Family Dynamics** – Potential for conflict among siblings or heirs, especially if not all want to be involved.
Continuity & Stability – Employees, customers, and community often appreciate that the company remains under family ownership.	**Capability Risk** – Success depends on whether family members truly have (or can be trained in) the skills for management, leadership, and ownership.
Tax Advantages – Estate planning strategies can help reduce taxes and protect family wealth.	**Illiquidity** – Family members often lack the funds to buy the business outright, requiring seller financing or creative deal structures.

Motivated Successors – Family members are usually highly invested in the business's success and continuation.

Lower Valuation – Internal transfers (like family transitions) typically use "fair market value" rather than competitive market bidding, often resulting in a lower sale price.

More Control Over Transition – Owner can plan a gradual transfer, mentor successors, and shape the long-term path.

Tradition Over Strategy – Desire to keep the business in the family may outweigh sound financial or strategic decisions.

2. Management Buyout (MBO)

A management buyout (MBO) is an internal exit strategy where a company's existing management team purchases the business from the owner. Rather than selling to outside buyers, the transition keeps leadership in place and leverages the managers' deep knowledge of the business.

Key characteristics include:

- **Financing Structure:** MBOs typically require significant seller financing, where the exiting owner provides part of the funding, combined with loans or outside capital (sometimes even private equity support).

- **Continuity:** Since the buyers are already running day-to-day operations, this option preserves company culture, customer relationships, and institutional knowledge.

- **Risks:** Challenges arise if the management team lacks true entrepreneurial skill. While they may be good operators, ownership requires additional risk-taking and leadership capacity. There's also the risk of "management sandbagging" (intentionally underperforming to lower the sale price).

- **Valuation & Liquidity:** Because it's not marketed to external bidders, the sale price may be lower than an external sale. The deal terms can also be less attractive for the seller, who often remains financially tied to the business for years.

In short, a management buyout allows for continuity and cultural stability, but it often comes with financial risk for the seller and depends heavily on the management team's ability to shift from employees to true owners.

Pros	Cons
Continuity – Keeps the business in familiar hands; management already knows operations, culture, and customers.	**Seller Financing** Risk – Owners often must finance a large portion of the purchase, tying up capital and extending financial risk.
Motivated Buyers – Managers usually have a strong desire to own and grow the business, leading to a highly invested buyer group.	Management Capability **Gap** – Good managers aren't always good entrepreneurs; ownership requires new skills in risk-taking and leadership.

Preserves Culture –
Employees and customers
often experience minimal
disruption, since leadership
remains consistent.

Potential for Sandbagging –
Managers may deliberately
underperform before the
buyout to reduce the
company's valuation.

Planned Transition – Can
be structured gradually,
giving the owner time to
mentor and prepare managers
for ownership.

Illiquidity – Management
teams usually lack
significant capital, making
external financing and seller
concessions necessary.

**Employee & Knowledge
Retention –** Retains
institutional expertise and
continuity for customers and
stakeholders.

Lower Price – Because it's
not a competitive market
sale, valuations are typically
lower and deal terms less
favorable for the seller.

3. Employee Stock Ownership Plan (ESOP)

An Employee Stock Ownership Plan (ESOP) is an internal exit strategy that transitions ownership of a business to its employees through a qualified retirement plan. Instead of selling to outside buyers, the company sets up a trust that acquires shares from the owner on behalf of employees.

Key characteristics include:

- **Ownership Structure:** The company borrows funds to buy the owner's shares, then contributes those shares into the ESOP trust for employees.

- **Employee Benefit:** Employees become beneficial owners, which can increase loyalty, motivation, and a sense of shared success.

- **Tax Advantages:** ESOPs often carry significant tax benefits. Sellers may defer capital gains in some cases, and shares are purchased with pre-tax dollars.
- **Continuity:** This option keeps the business in its "extended family," preserving culture and continuity while spreading ownership across employees.
- **Complexity & Cost:** ESOPs are heavily regulated, require ongoing compliance, and can be expensive to establish and administer. The company is also obligated to repurchase shares from departing employees, creating long-term financial commitments.

In short, an ESOP provides a way for owners to exit gradually, reward employees, and gain tax advantages, it requires strong management systems and the ability to handle regulatory and financial complexity.

Pros	Cons
Employee Ownership – Creates broad-based ownership, turning employees into stakeholders with a vested interest in company success.	**Complex & Expensive** – ESOPs are complicated to establish and require ongoing regulatory compliance and legal oversight.
Tax Advantages – Sellers may defer capital gains, and shares are purchased with pre-tax dollars, creating potential savings.	**Repurchase Obligation** – The company must buy back shares when employees leave, creating long-term financial commitments.

Pros	Cons
Employee Ownership – Creates broad-based ownership, turning employees into stakeholders with a vested interest in company success.	**Complex & Expensive –** ESOPs are complicated to establish and require ongoing regulatory compliance and legal oversight.
Continuity & Culture – Keeps the business in the "extended family," preserving company culture, employee morale, and loyalty.	**Requires Strong Management** – An ESOP only works if the business has a capable management team; owners cannot rely on employees alone to lead.
Gradual Exit – Allows owners to sell their shares over time, providing flexibility rather than requiring an immediate full sale.	**Not a Clean Break** – Owners often remain tied to the business financially and operationally for a period after establishing the ESOP.
Employee Motivation – Aligns employees' incentives with business performance, encouraging them to "think like owners."	**Suitability Limits** – Generally best for mid-sized companies with strong, sustainable cash flow; not always viable for smaller or less stable firms.

External Strategies
4. Strategic Buyer (Synergy Buyer)

Selling to a strategic buyer (often called a synergy buyer) is an external exit strategy where the business is sold to a competitor or a company in a related industry that sees unique value in acquiring it. Unlike financial buyers, who focus primarily on investment returns, strategic buyers look for synergies—ways the acquisition will strengthen their existing operations.

Key characteristics include:

- **Synergy Value:** Strategic buyers often pay a premium because they can reduce costs or increase revenue by combining operations (e.g., eliminating redundant staff, expanding product lines, or gaining geographic reach).

- **Integration Challenges:** While synergies create value, they may also lead to layoffs or cultural clashes, as overlapping positions and systems are consolidated.

- **Higher Valuations:** Since strategic buyers see more immediate financial benefit, they're often willing to offer higher purchase prices than family transfers, MBOs, or ESOPs.

- **Legacy Concerns:** Owners may worry whether employees will be retained, whether the business will remain in the same community, and how the buyer's culture will impact the company's legacy.

- **Faster Exits:** External sales like this usually close more quickly than internal strategies, though owners may still need to remain involved during a transition period.

In short, a strategic buyer is attractive because they often pay more and move quickly, the trade-offs include potential cultural disruption, employee layoffs, and less control over the company's long-term legacy.

Pros	Cons
Higher Valuation – Strategic buyers often pay a premium because they can achieve synergies such as eliminating redundancies, scaling operations, or expanding product lines.	**Cultural Integration Risks –** Differences in company culture may create friction, leading to challenges for employees and customers.
Faster Exit – These deals typically close more quickly than internal transfers (family, MBO, ESOP).	**Employee Impact** – Redundant roles are often eliminated, which can cause layoffs and affect morale.
Financial Strength – Strategic buyers usually have greater resources and can pay more cash upfront compared to internal successors.	**Legacy Concerns** – The business may be relocated, rebranded, or absorbed into the buyer's operations, which may conflict with the owner's desire to preserve their legacy.

Growth Opportunities – The acquiring company may provide expanded market reach, geographic coverage, or product synergies that accelerate growth.

Reduced Control – Once sold, the original owner typically has little influence over how employees, customers, or community relationships are managed.

Clear Buyer Motivation – Strategic buyers are motivated by specific synergies, making negotiations more straightforward and value-driven.

Owner Involvement – Some strategic buyers may still require the owner to remain temporarily during integration, which can be emotionally challenging.

5. Private Equity/Financial Buyer

A Private Equity (PE) or financial buyer is an external exit strategy where an investment firm purchases a business with the primary goal of generating financial returns. Unlike strategic buyers, who seek operational synergies, financial buyers focus on value creation through growth, restructuring, or future resale.

Key characteristics include:

- **Investment Focus:** PE firms typically buy businesses to improve operations, grow revenue, and later sell at a profit. They view acquisitions as financial assets rather than long-term legacy holdings.

- **Deal Structure:** Transactions often involve the owner rolling over equity (keeping a minority stake). This creates the potential for a "second bite of the apple," where the owner profits again when the PE firm later sells the business.

- **Professional Management:** PE buyers bring in experienced management and operational systems, which can professionalize and scale the business.

- **Owner Involvement:** Sellers are often expected to stay involved for a transition period, either as consultants or minority partners.

- **Growth-Oriented:** PE firms typically look for businesses with strong potential for expansion, recurring revenues, or operational improvements.

In short, a financial buyer can provide liquidity, growth capital, and another chance to profit, but it may require continued owner involvement and may lead to a culture shift focused more on returns than legacy.

Pros	Cons
High Growth Potential – PE firms often bring capital, expertise, and operational improvements to grow and scale the business.	**Owner Involvement** – Most deals require the owner to stay engaged for a period (as a consultant, manager, or minority partner), limiting an immediate exit.

Liquidity with Upside – Owners may sell a majority stake while keeping some equity, creating the chance for a "second bite of the apple" when the firm later sells the business.

Culture Shift – PE buyers are focused on financial returns, which can alter company culture and priorities, sometimes at odds with legacy goals.

Professional Management – Brings in systems, structure, and experienced executives to professionalize operations.

Pressure for Performance – Expectation of rapid growth and profitability can create stress for management and employees.

Capital Infusion – Provides growth capital to expand product lines, markets, or acquisitions.

Loss of Control – Once the deal closes, owners typically lose decision-making authority and may have limited influence on company direction.

Attractive Valuation – Often competitive with strategic buyers, especially for businesses with strong recurring revenues and growth potential.

Not Legacy-Focused – PE buyers rarely prioritize keeping the business in the community or preserving the founder's long-term vision.

Exit Strategy Comparison:
Internal vs. External Paths

Strategy	Pros	Cons
Family Transfer	<ul><li>Preserves legacy and keeps the business in the family</li><li>Continuity for employees and community</li><li>Estate and tax planning opportunities</li><li>Motivated successors</li></ul>	<ul><li>Family conflict and dynamics</li><li>Successors may lack capability</li><li>Requires seller financing/gradual transition</li><li>Lower valuation vs. external sale</li></ul>
Management Buyout (MBO)	<ul><li>Keeps leadership and culture intact</li><li>Motivated and knowledgeable buyers</li><li>Planned transition with continuity for employees</li></ul>	<ul><li>Heavy reliance on seller financing</li><li>Managers may lack entrepreneurial skills</li><li>Risk of management sandbagging</li><li>Lower price than external sale</li></ul>

Strategy	Pros	Cons
Employee Stock Ownership Plan (ESOP)	▪ Broad employee ownership builds loyalty ▪ Significant tax advantages ▪ Preserves culture and continuity ▪ Allows gradual exit	▪ Complex and expensive to establish ▪ Requires strong management team ▪ Ongoing repurchase obligations ▪ Not a clean break for the seller
Strategic Buyer (Synergy Buyer)	▪ Often pays the highest price ▪ Faster exit compared to internal transfers ▪ Cash-rich buyers with clear synergies ▪ Growth opportunities via integration	▪ Employee layoffs from redundancies ▪ Cultural integration risks ▪ Legacy concerns (relocation, rebrand, community impact) ▪ Limited control post-sale

Strategy	Pros	Cons
Private Equity / Financial Buyer	▪ Provides liquidity with chance for "second bite of the apple" ▪ Growth capital and professional management ▪ Attractive valuations for scalable businesses	Requires owner involvement post-sale Focus on financial returns, not legacy Loss of control once deal closes Cultural shift and performance pressure

Valuation Differences by Strategy

Each exit strategy will present its own range of values for the exit. If you're doing a family transfer or an ESOP, because it's not actually being marketed to an outside buyer, the IRS requires you to use fair market valuation methodology, which may not necessarily be the highest value versus a competitive bidding process if you go to market.

When you go to market, you have several buyers looking at it through a different lens from a value standpoint and from an investment standpoint as far as return on investment. A competitor who wants to buy knows immediately they're going to come in; take over your client book; reduce or eliminate your payroll department, HR, and your administrative back office; and save all that money. There may be other inefficiencies in operations that present expense reduction or increased revenue. So they may be willing to pay you more because they're going to value it differently.

When finding the right exit strategy for a business owner, we consider a few different things:

- What do those deal structures look like from a net return?
- Do they help you accomplish all your financial goals and priorities?
- What feelings do each exit strategy prompt in you?

Most business owners I've met have had their own idea of how they'd like to exit. Our goal is not to tell you what exit strategy to use. We want you to explore all the exit strategies and have those conversations. We don't want you to be one of the seventy percent of business owners who are not satisfied within one year of their exit, and seventy-eight percent who fail the first time they go to market. Our goal is to have you exit the business according to your ideal exit and on your terms. Once you identify the exit strategy or strategies, you're going to start to manage toward that exit to maximize value.

"Planning is bringing the future into the present so that you can do something about it now." – Alan Lakein

Chapter Four in Practice

Reflection Questions

- Which exit strategy aligns best with your values and goals?

- Have you had honest conversations with potential internal successors about their true interest and capability?

- What are the emotional factors most important to you in your exit?

- Are you prepared for the reality that you may not receive 100 percent at closing?

Action Step

After reviewing all five exit strategies, identify the top two that make the most sense for your situation.

CHAPTER FIVE

Creating a Transferable Business

Would you buy your company without you running it?

❧

The real test of a business's value comes down to one simple question: **Would you buy your company if you weren't the one running it the next day?**

For many owners, the honest answer is no. The company's success depends too heavily on their daily decisions, relationships, and problem-solving. While that may have worked during the building years, it becomes a liability when it's time to exit. Buyers aren't purchasing the owner. They're purchasing a company that can run without the owner. If the business cannot operate independently, its value plummets.

A Case Study:
The Overextended Juggler

Take the story of Mark, owner of a thriving regional contracting company. Mark prided himself on his ability to keep every plate spinning. He was the one who landed big contracts, approved every major purchase, and personally handled client relationships. From the outside, his company looked strong. but when the potential buyer began due diligence, cracks appeared.

Every major decision required Mark's approval. Without him present, projects slowed. Financial records were incomplete because only Mark understood the "system" he had in his head.

41

His managers were loyal, but not empowered. The buyer realized that acquiring the company meant acquiring Mark—and Mark was planning to leave.

The deal collapsed.

That moment became a turning point. Mark realized that a successful business is not the same thing as a transferable business. Buyers aren't just purchasing revenue or assets; they're purchasing **transferable value,** which is the assurance that the company will thrive without the owner.

Creating a transferable business requires intentional design. It means building systems, teams, and strategies that inspire confidence in a buyer. It also means eliminating risks that could cause them to hesitate, reduce their offer, or walk away altogether.

Mark's wake-up call was painful, but it became the turning point. With guidance, he began to document processes, empower managers, and build repeatable systems. Over two years, the company shifted from a founder-dependent enterprise to a transferable business. When he went back to market, buyers saw not just a business, but an organization ready to thrive without its owner.

Transferable Value Indicators

Buyers evaluate businesses through specific drivers of transferable value. Each one directly impacts how much they are willing to pay and how much of that payment is guaranteed at closing versus held back in contingencies.

1. Qualified, Invested Management Team and Key Employees

A strong management team is one of the most powerful indicators of transferable value. Buyers want to see a business that can operate independently of the owner.

Questions to consider:

- How does decision-making work today?
- Have you delegated authority, or are managers just carrying out orders?
- Do your key people have the skills and autonomy to run the business when you step away?

If your team is engaged, skilled, and invested in the company's success, the business is far more attractive and less risky.

2. Consistent, Sustainable Profits and Cash Flow

Buyers pay more for stability. A well-documented history of profitability builds trust, while predictive models create confidence about the future. Recurring revenues like contracts, subscriptions, or long-term service agreements are particularly valuable because they are less risky than one-time sales.

Questions to consider:

- Have you tracked the history of your financial performance?
- Can you show models that project future stability?

- Do you have recurring revenue streams, or only recurring transactions?

3. Documented Growth Strategy

A clear roadmap of where the company has been, where it is now, and where it is going reassures buyers that opportunity lies ahead. A documented growth plan gives the next owner something to step into, not something to reinvent.

Questions to consider:

- Can you show a proven history of growth?
- Do you have a written plan that outlines future opportunities?

4. Investment in High-Performing Technology, Equipment, and Facilities

Modern infrastructure signals efficiency and competitiveness. Outdated systems, on the other hand, lower value because buyers see immediate expenses after closing.

Questions to consider:

- Have you kept technology, equipment, and facilities current?
- Will the new owner need to invest heavily on day one?

5. Internal Systems, Processes, and Procedures

Processes that are documented and consistently followed reduce dependence on the owner and allow for scalability. If everything lives in your head, buyers see risk.

Questions to consider:

- Are your systems written down and consistently applied?
- Can new employees be trained quickly?
- Are processes replicable as the company grows?

6. Niche Products and Services

Companies with unique offerings and a clear niche are harder to replicate, making them more valuable. Differentiation creates resilience and attracts buyers who see growth potential.

Questions to consider:

- What makes you different from competitors?
- How are your offerings designed for long-term growth?

7. High Customer and Supply Chain Diversification

Over-reliance on a few customers or suppliers creates fragility. If one relationship fails, revenue and operations suffer. Buyers often reduce their offer or structure earnouts if too much depends on a handful of relationships.

Questions to consider:

- Do you have a broad, stable customer base?

- Are your suppliers diversified, or do you depend on a single source?

8. Transferable Customer Contracts

Customer contracts that transfer to new ownership create confidence in continued revenue. Without transferability clauses, customers can walk away at closing, reducing value.

Questions to consider:

- Do your contracts include transfer provisions?

- Are agreements long-term or at-will relationships that could disappear?

Transferable Value Indicators vs. Company-Specific Risks

Transferable Value Indicator (Strength)	Company-Specific Risk (Weakness)
Qualified, Invested Management Team – Skilled leaders who can make decisions, run operations, and stay engaged post-owner.	**Unskilled, Non-Invested Management Team** – Wrong people in key roles, no leadership development, heavy dependence on owner.

Consistent, SustainableProfits and Cash Flow – Reliable financial history, recurring revenues, strong future projections.

Lack of Financial Systems, Controls, and Performance Metrics – Poor reporting, weak controls, no credible forecasts, limited buyer confidence.

Documented Growth Strategy – Clear roadmap of past, present, and future growth that buyers can step into.

Undocumented Processes – Critical knowledge stuck in owner's head; no scalable, repeatable systems for new hires or growth.

Investment in High-Performing Technology, Equipment, and Facilities – Modern, efficient infrastructure with no looming replacement costs.

Outdated Equipment and Facilities – Immediate capital needs for upgrades lower purchase price and slow growth potential.

Internal Systems, Processes, and Procedures – Well-documented, consistently followed systems that create efficiency and scalability.

Undocumented Processes – Ad hoc operations, inconsistencies, and dependence on the owner prevent smooth transfer. *(overlaps with Growth Strategy risk)*

Niche Products and Services – Unique offerings that differentiate the business from competitors and support long-term growth.

Cultural and Performance Issues – Lack of alignment, accountability, or clarity around value proposition; weak culture undermines execution.

High Customer/Supply Chain Diversification – Wide base of customers and suppliers, lowering dependence on a few relationships.

Supply Chain Risk – Over-reliance on one customer or supplier; disruption or loss of a key relationship can sharply reduce revenue.

Transferable Customer Contracts – Contracts that explicitly carry over to new ownership, ensuring revenue continuity.

Customer/Revenue Concentration Risk – Customers free to walk if contracts aren't transferable; value reduced through holdbacks or earnouts.

The formula is simple:

- **More transferable value = Higher price, more cash at closing, less reliance on contingencies**
- **More company-specific risk = Lower price, reduced certainty, more earnouts and holdbacks**

Mark learned this lesson the hard way. His first attempt to sell failed because risks outweighed value. By addressing leadership gaps, documenting systems, diversifying customers, and upgrading equipment, he turned his business into a transferable asset. When he went back to market, buyers saw an organization ready to thrive without him.

The Owner Dependence Index Assessment

As an owner, how involved are you in the business? How dependent is the business on you in key areas? We have our clients take a test to get a measurement of how involved they are in these eight key areas:

1. **Internal Operations** - Day-to-day business operations and processes

2. **Strategy Planning** - Long-term planning and strategic direction

3. **Governance** - Board oversight and corporate governance

4. **Ownership Structure** - Equity arrangements and ownership decisions

5. **Financial Matters** - Financial management and reporting

6. **Performance Management** - Employee evaluation and development

7. **Sales and Business Development** - Revenue generation and client relationships

8. **Company Culture** - Organizational culture and employee engagement

Then we ask, "What can you start delegating today? Who do you need to hire to lower the score of your involvement in each of these areas?" At the end of this chapter, there's a short test called the Owner Dependence Index Assessment (ODIA). This helps us dive deeper into those questions and determine what can be done to change those dynamics within their own company.

Managing Toward Your Chosen Exit Strategy

Once you've identified the exit path that best fits your goals, the real work begins: managing your business with that end in mind. Too many companies plateau because the owner refuses to let go. Without delegation to capable leaders, growth stalls, and the business remains dependent on the person who built it. That dependence not only limits growth, it limits value.

Managing toward your chosen strategy is also about continuity and protection. Your business should be transferable not only for a sale, but also in the event of death, disability, divorce, or partnership dissolution. Just as succession planning in wealth management protects assets for heirs, exit planning protects the continuity and value of your company for employees, family, and stakeholders.

If your strategy is an ESOP, the question becomes, who will lead once you step away? You are not the next CEO. In fact, it may take five to six years to identify, train, and transition the right leader to take over. If your strategy involves family succession, ask "are they truly ready? Do they need development or coaching?

How will the deal be structured, especially if you are financing part of it yourself?"

If your exit involves selling to private equity or a strategic buyer, preparation looks different. Investment bankers will quickly identify what matters to those buyers, whether that's inventory levels, customer concentration, geography, or margin consistency. They know what red flags reduce value and what strengths attract different buyers.

The most effective way to prepare is to look at your business through a buyer's eyes. Ask yourself: "If I were buying this company, what would concern me?" Owners already do this for customers by constantly adapting offerings based on what clients want. The same perspective shift is required when preparing for buyers.

The less the business depends on you, the more attractive it becomes. Transferability increases buyer confidence, expands the pool of interested parties, and creates competition. That competition often drives better deal structures and higher valuations.

When you manage intentionally toward your exit strategy, you're not only increasing the financial value of your company, you're also securing its future for employees, heirs, and stakeholders. A transferable business positions you to exit on your terms.

"Have a bias towards action—let's see something happen now. You can break that big plan into small steps and take the first step right away." – Indira Gandhi

Chapter Five in Practice

Reflection Questions

- Would you buy your company without you running it the next day?

- Which of the transferable value indicators are strong in your business today? Which are weak?

- Where does your business carry the most risk: management, finances, culture, customers, or suppliers?

- Do your customer contracts transfer to new ownership or are they vulnerable at closing?

- What steps can you take this year to increase transferability and reduce risk?

Action Step

1. Scan the QR code below and take the Owner Dependence Index assessment to measure your current involvement in the eight critical business areas.

2. Identify the top three areas where you can begin delegating responsibilities or need to hire additional team members.

3. Create a 90-day plan to reduce your involvement scores in these priority areas.

Scan this QR code to take the Owner
Dependence Index assessment:

CHAPTER SIX

Why You Should Start Exit Planning Now

The Myth of the Easy Exit and the Five-Year Problem

❧

Every business owner believes deep down that when the time comes, they'll be able to sell quickly, profitably, and on their terms. The reality, however, is far different. Successful exits don't "just happen." They're the result of careful planning, long-term preparation, and deliberate action. Yet two powerful illusions hold owners back: the myth of the easy exit and the five-year problem.

The Myth of the Easy Exit

The myth of the easy exit whispers that selling a business is straightforward: find a buyer, sign the paperwork, cash the check. But behind every story of a seemingly effortless sale is a reality filled with complexity. Owners often see only the outcome of someone else's transaction and not the years of preparation it required. Did you know seventy percent of business transfers fail on the first attempt to sell the business?

No exit is easy. Negotiations are complex, due diligence is demanding, and emotions run high. Without preparation, even attractive offers can collapse under scrutiny. Believing otherwise creates a dangerous complacency. Owners assume everything will fall into place when the time is right, only to discover too late that they aren't ready, their business isn't transferable, and the opportunity has passed them by.

Understanding investment banking business models is important as well. They want to prepare your business to go to market and sell in the next six to nine months. They review hundreds of potential businesses to sell every year. They turn down seven out of ten businesses to sell. Why? There are many factors, but the top reasons are the business financials are not ready to go through due diligence, the business is not transferable as discussed earlier, and the business owners value expectations are not realistic.

The Five-Year Problem

Ask a business owner when they plan to exit, and the most common answer is *"in five years."*

Here's the problem: Five years rarely means five years. It's often a form of avoidance, a safe answer that pushes the decision far enough into the future to remove urgency. Most owners plan one to three years ahead in their business, not five. So when they say five years, what they really mean is "not now."

The five-year answer becomes a moving target. Ask the same question five years later, and the answer is often the same: "Five years from now." The risk is clear—an exit that never actually gets planned. Then life steps in with its own deadlines: illness, disability, burnout, or market changes that leave no time for preparation.

The solution is simple, though not easy: **Start today.** Even if you don't intend to sell for years, the discipline of planning now ensures you are prepared when the time comes.

Timing in the marketplace is unpredictable. Entire industries experience waves of consolidation, where private equity firms or strategic buyers roll up companies in a sector. During these periods, multiples spike.

I once met an IT business owner who was offered a multiple nearly double the industry norm. The offer was extraordinary, driven by both geography and timing. The buyer needed a presence in his city and wanted to close quickly. The owner wasn't ready. The offer could not maintain his lifestyle, and mentally, at forty-eight, he couldn't picture life after the business. The opportunity slipped by.

We've seen the same trend in HVAC, dental, and veterinary practices. Private equity enters, valuations soar, then the window closes. Owners who are ready capture the upside. Those who don't miss it. The market rewards readiness.

The Three-Part Framework for Exit Planning

Every owner's situation is unique, preparation often revolves around three key areas:

1. **Financial Objectives – Liquidity Creation:** Your business equity is illiquid. Exit planning is about turning that equity into cash to support retirement, lifestyle, heirs, and charitable goals. Determine how much you need to net to achieve these objectives. Few owners can answer this with precision, clarity in this step is the foundation of readiness.

2. **Business Transition – Removing Yourself:** The business must operate without you. This means gradually reducing owner dependence, empowering leadership, and

ensuring continuity. Exit planning provides a roadmap for how to step away without weakening the company you worked so hard to build.

3. **Legacy Planning – Wealth and Impact Management:** For many, the exit creates generational wealth for the first time. With it comes responsibility. How will this wealth affect your children? Will it empower or burden them? Do you want to support community causes? Do you want to structure philanthropy pre-sale, post-sale, or through estate planning? These questions move exit planning beyond numbers into purpose.

Why do owners delay? At the core, it's emotional. Planning feels like admitting that something you love is coming to an end. But it is not the end. It's about shifting energy into a new pursuit.

Some owners describe the daily "chemical high" of running a business, like the adrenaline that comes from solving problems and driving growth. Letting go feels like losing that energy. The key is not to stop; it's to redirect. Exit planning helps you find what will replace that sense of purpose and excitement.

Remember, having an exit strategy does not mean you must sell today. It means that when opportunity knocks—or when the unexpected happens—you are ready. Without it, heirs may be forced to sell quickly, often at a discount. With it, your business maintains value, your employees are protected, and your family is secure.

Exit planning should not be viewed as an ending. It's a transition to what's next. When approached correctly, it allows you to remove the negatives of ownership—the stress, the constant demands, the risks—while stepping into something positive and rewarding.

What do you want to replace your business with? A new venture? Philanthropy? More time with family? Travel? Mentoring? Without this vision, owners avoid planning because they fear a void. With it, planning becomes an energizing opportunity to shape the next chapter.

Stephen Covey's advice rings true here: "Begin with the end in mind." Exit planning is the discipline of managing toward your desired future. It balances both the emotional and the technical sides of transition:

- **The Emotional Side:** addressing identity, purpose, family dynamics, and legacy.
- **The Technical Side:** building transferable value, structuring deals, maximizing net proceeds, and protecting wealth.

Owners who succeed address both. Those who don't will struggle.

Final Chapter in Practice

Final Reflection Questions

- What emotional factors are preventing you from starting exit planning?
- What would your ideal day look like one year after your exit?

- Who are the key people (family, employees, advisors) you need to have conversations with?
- What's your biggest fear about exiting your business, and how can planning address it?

Your Next Steps

1. Take the Business Exit Readiness Index and Owner Dependence Index assessments if you haven't already.

2. Begin conversations with family members or key employees about their interests and capabilities.

3. Identify and begin building your advisory team (CPA, attorney, exit planner, investment banker).

4. Start documenting your business processes and developing your management team.

Create a preliminary timeline for your ideal exit (even if it's five to ten years out).

CONCLUSION

Exiting on Your Terms

❧

"First comes thought: then organization of that thought, into ideas and plans; then transformation of those plans into reality. The beginning, as you observe, is in your imagination."

– Napoleon Hill

Exit planning is a safeguard. It ensures that when the time arrives to pass the company on, you do so with clarity rather than chaos. Without preparation, even the strongest business can lose value quickly. Key employees leave, customers lose confidence, and families are left with hard decisions they are unprepared to make. With preparation, those same challenges transform into opportunities. Value is preserved, transitions are smooth, and the owner departs with dignity and control.

Planning ahead allows an owner to move from reaction to intention. Instead of being forced into hurried negotiations or fire-sale conditions, you can shape the terms of your departure. You decide whether the next chapter of the company belongs to family, employees, or an outside buyer. You decide whether wealth created in the business supports retirement, philanthropy, or the next generation.

The true power of exit planning lies in alignment. It aligns the company's operations with the expectations of future owners. It aligns the owner's personal goals with the realities of market timing. And it aligns the legacy of the business with the values of the person who built it.

An exit will come, whether you prepare for it or not. The question is whether it will unfold by accident or by design. Business owners who begin the process early create options, maximize outcomes, and ensure continuity for those who depend on them. Those who wait leave their future to chance.

Exit planning is how you turn years of effort into a legacy that endures. The future you imagine becomes possible the moment you plan for it.

www.ingramcontent.com/pod-product-compliance
Lightning Source LLC
Chambersburg PA
CBHW071609200326

41519CB00021BB/6939